FANTASTIC FLIGHT

CONTENTS

JAMES BURNETT
CALVIN IRONS

FEATHERED FLIGHT

The first airplane flight occurred less than 100 years ago, but birds and their ancestors have been performing fantastic flying feats for millions of years.

The Snow Goose

Snow geese are migrating birds. After breeding in the Arctic, they fly south to spend winter in the warmth of California and the Gulf of Mexico.

A flock of snow geese flies in a V-shape. This helps the birds to fly against the wind – and to avoid colliding with one another.

A Full Grown Snow Goose

Length: $26\frac{1}{2} - 33\frac{1}{2}$ inches

Wingspan: $52\frac{3}{4} - 66$ inches

Weight: $5 - 8$ pounds

Speed: up to 45 miles per hour

The Wandering Albatross

A Full Grown Wandering Albatross

Length: $3\frac{1}{2} - 4\frac{1}{2}$ feet

Wingspan: 9 – 11 feet

Weight: $15\frac{1}{2} - 26\frac{1}{2}$ pounds

Speed: 50 miles per hour

The wingspan of the wandering albatross is the largest of any bird in the world. In flight over the sea, albatrosses can soar gracefully, but on land they waddle awkwardly and even trip over their own feet. Early sailors called these clumsy creatures "goony birds."

The Bee Hummingbird

A Full Grown Bee Hummingbird

Length: $2\frac{1}{2}$ inches

Wingspan: $2\frac{3}{4}$ inches

Weight: $\frac{1}{16}$ of an ounce

Speed: 50 – 60 miles per hour

The bee hummingbird is the smallest bird in the world. Hummingbirds' wings beat up to 200 times per second – so quickly that you can hardly see them.

3

WINGS AND WEIGHTS

Look at the birds and measurements shown on pages 2–5.

1. Which birds have a wingspan of:
   a. less than one yard?
   How much less?
   b. more than three yards?
   How much more?
2. Which birds weigh:
   a. less than one ounce?
   b. less than one pound?
3. Which two birds have the least difference in:
   a. weight?
   b. wingspan?

A Mute Swan

Wingspan: 7 feet, 5 inches

Weight: 22 pounds

Quail

Wingspan: 14 inches
Weight: $4\frac{1}{4}$ ounces

Peregrine Falcon

Wingspan: 3 feet, 3 inches
Weight: 2 pounds, 13 ounces

Buzzard

Wingspan: 4 feet, 3 inches
Weight: 3 pounds

- The fastest bird is the peregrine falcon. Diving from the sky, peregrine falcons can reach speeds of more than 160 miles per hour.
- The heaviest bird of flight is the kori bustard. See if you can find out how much it weighs.

How do you compare?
- Which bird's wingspan is closest to your height?
- How many of your handspans would fit along the wingspan of a wandering albatross?

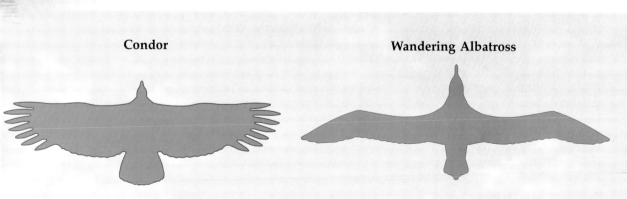

Condor

Wingspan: 10 feet
Weight: 31 pounds

Wandering Albatross

Wingspan: 11 feet
Weight: 26 $\frac{1}{2}$ pounds

DAY DREAMERS

People have always dreamed of flying like the birds. The first designers of "flying machines" tried to copy birds' flapping wings – but none of their amazing machines ever flew.

The famous Italian artist Leonardo da Vinci made the first scientific study of bird flight. In 1485, he planned a bird-like flying machine. It was designed to be powered by a person using pedals, pulleys, and ropes. It was never built.

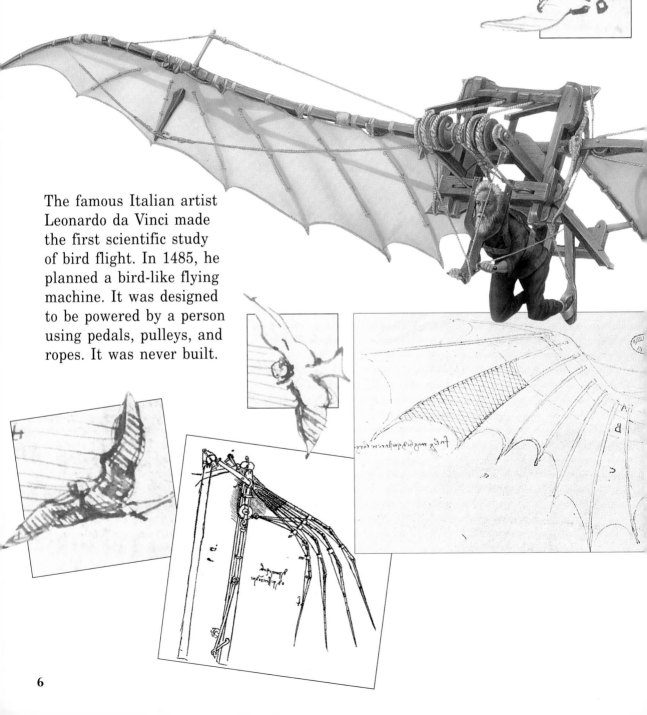

The Flying Duck

In 1678, a French locksmith built a machine that had arms designed to paddle up and down like a duck's feet. The "flying duck" never got off the ground.

Tower Jumpers

Some early attempts at flight were made by people who attached fragile, feathered wings to their arms. They jumped from towers, flapping madly in a desperate and dangerous attempt to fly.

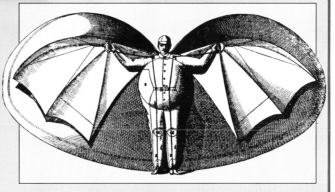

ON A SMALL SCALE

Leonardo da Vinci made many sketches of birds in flight. He was careful to show the real thing as accurately as possible.

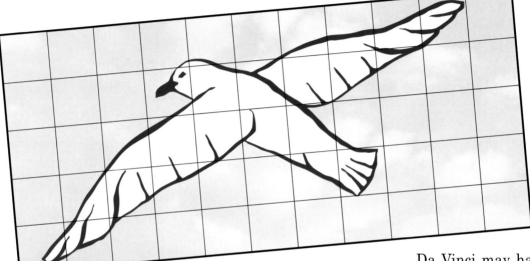

1. Find or draw a grid that has one-inch squares. On your grid, draw a bird like the one above. Make sure it measures the same number of squares.

2. Measure the length of the bird above. Then measure the length of your bird. What did you notice?

3. Follow the steps on page 9 to make a glider.

4. Suppose you made a glider that was half the size of the one shown on the grid on page 9. How long would its body be? How high would its body be?

Da Vinci may have use grids to help him mak accurate drawings. By copying a sketch from one grid onto a grid with larger squares, h could have made accurate enlargements of his drawings.

A Paper Glider

You will need:

> a piece of heavy paper, at least 9 inches x 10 inches;
> scissors; ruler; tape; a coin.

Step 1: Fold the paper in half.

Step 2: Double all the measurements of this glider outline. Use a grid to help you if you wish. Draw the larger outline on your paper, with the bottom of the glider on the folded edge.

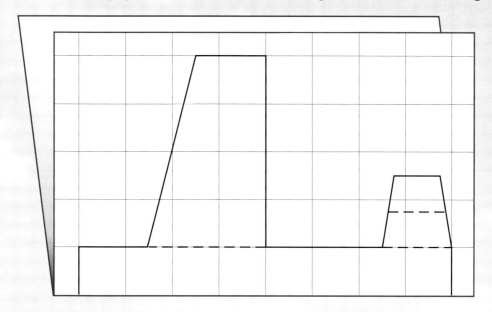

Step 3: Cut out your glider. Don't cut along the fold.

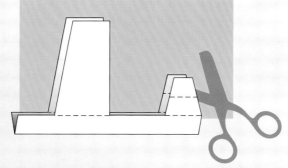

Step 4: Fold the wings and tail as shown below. Then attach a coin to the nose.

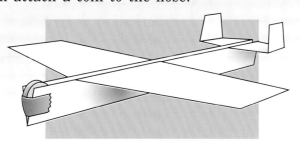

KEEN ON KITES

Kites were the first flying machines that really worked. For centuries, people all over the world have made kites for fun. Some special kites led the way for the design of the first airplanes.

Hargrave's Box Kites

In 1894, the Australian Lawrence Hargrave built four large box-shaped kites. Together they lifted him 16 feet into the air. The wings on many of the first airplanes were based on his successful designs.

People from many cultures use kites in festivals and other celebrations.

Kites were used in China more than 2,000 years ago. Much later, the explorer Marco Polo reported that the Chinese used huge kites to carry people up into the sky to inspect the land below.

KITE DESIGN

Kites can have all kinds of colors and patterns, but most importantly they need to be designed to fly well.

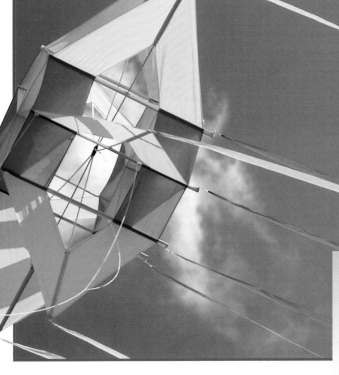

DID YOU KNOW?

Sometimes more than one kite is attached to a single line. The record number of kites to be flown on one line is 11,284. This fantastic flight took place in October 1990.

Research

- Find out about some famous people who experimented with kites. You could start with Benjamin Franklin, Alexander Graham Bell, or the Wright brothers.
- List any records you can find about kites and kite flying.

1. Look at the kites in the photo above.

   a. Write some words to describe the shape of the kites.

   b. Write what you know about the angles of the corners.

   c. Write about the diagonals. Which diagonal is also a line of symmetry?

2. Look at the photo of the kite on page 12.

   a. Write a list of the shapes you can see in this kite.

   b. Describe some ways in which triangles are used in the kite.

3. Write a description of the patterns you can see in the dragon kite.

BEAUTIFUL BALLOONS

If you fill a balloon with hot air it will rise. Large hot-air balloons can lift heavy loads. The first passenger flight in a hot-air balloon took place more than 200 years ago.

Two Frenchmen, Joseph and Etienne Montgolfier, noticed that a silk garment tended to rise as it dried above a hot stove. This gave them the idea for a hot-air balloon. They made a huge balloon from cloth and paper, and filled it with hot air produced by burning straw in a heavy burner.

The Montgolfier Balloon

First Flight Facts

Height of balloon: 70 feet

Maximum diameter: 46 feet

Volume: 77,700 cubic feet

Take-off weight: about 1,730 pounds

Altitude reached: 3,000 feet

Distance flown: 6 miles

Flight time: 25 minutes

The first passengers to fly in the Montgolfier balloon were a sheep, a duck, and a rooster. The first human passengers flew in the balloon on November 21, 1783.

Fact Sheet: a modern hot-air balloon

Height: 70 feet

Maximum diameter: 50 feet

Volume: 57,000 cubic feet

Take-off weight: up to 5,000 pounds

Maximum altitude: over 50,000 feet

Flight time: usually 1–2 hours

A large balloon festival occurs every October in Albuquerque, New Mexico. Balloons fill the sky to "dance" and take part in events such as a "balloon rodeo."

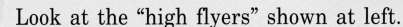

Up, Up, and Away

High Flyers

Gas-filled Balloon
113,740 feet

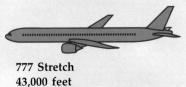

Hot-air Balloon
64,997 feet

777 Stretch
43,000 feet

Helicopter
40,820 feet

Ruppell's Vulture
37,000 feet

Look at the "high flyers" shown at left.

1. How much higher did the gas-filled balloon fly than:
   a. the 777 Stretch?
   b. the vulture?

2. Ten miles is 52,800 feet. Which high flyers have flown higher than:
   a. 10 miles?
   b. 20 miles?

3. What altitude did the Montgolfier balloon reach on its first flight? (See page 14.) How much higher than this has a hot-air balloon flown?

Ruppell's vultures are rarely seen above 20,000 feet. But on November 29, 1973, a Ruppell's vulture collided with a passenger aircraft flying over Africa at an altitude of 37,000 feet. This is the highest any bird has ever been known to fly.

Highest Mountain
Mt. Everest: 29,002 feet

Research

- The record for a balloon staying in the air is 144 hours. Find out how long other aircraft can stay in the air.
- Find out about weather balloons. How high do they fly? What data do they collect?

AWESOME AIRSHIPS

An airship is a very large balloon. Unlike a hot-air balloon, an airship uses its own power to move forward. Airships are slow aircraft. When they fly into a strong wind, they might not move at all!

The Goodyear Blimp

This "blimp" is used mainly for advertising. It also carries cameras to capture a bird's-eye view of sporting events.

Fact Sheet

Length: 192 feet

Maximum diameter: 59 feet

Volume: 202,700 cubic feet

Take-off weight: 12,320 pounds

Cruising altitude: 10,000 feet

Cruising speed: 50 miles per hour

Range: 500 miles

The Giffard Airship

The first airship was powered by a coal-burning steam engine. The inventor, Henri Giffard, flew his airship on September 24, 1852.

Try this problem:
Giffard's airship carried 500 pounds of coal, and the steam engine weighed 350 pounds. List the other parts of the airship and guess their weights. Use all this information to help you estimate the total take-off weight.

First Flight Facts

Airship length: 144 feet

Maximum diameter: 39 feet

Volume: 88,300 cubic feet

Take-off weight: unknown

Altitude reached: unknown

Cruising speed: 5 miles per hour

Distance flown: 17 miles

THE LONGEST AIRSHIP

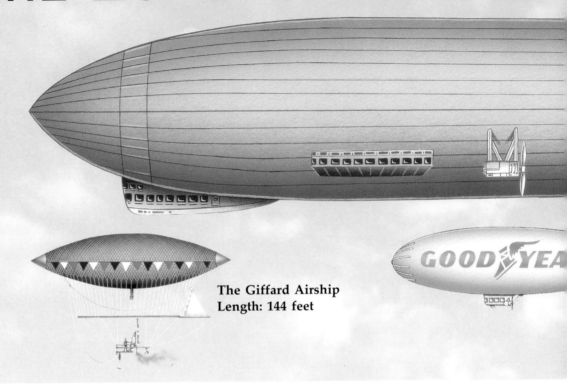

The Giffard Airship
Length: 144 feet

1. How much longer was the *Hindenburg* than:
   a. the Giffard airship?
   b. a 777 passenger plane?
2. How many Goodyear Blimps would fit along the length of the *Hindenburg*? How did you figure out the answer?
3. Measure the length of your classroom. How many times would your classroom fit along the length of:
   a. the *Hindenburg*?
   b. the Goodyear Blimp?
4. Think of some things that are about the same length as the *Hindenburg*. Write your ideas.

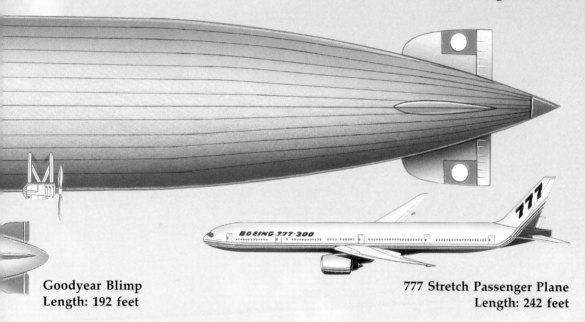

The Hindenburg Airship

Length: 804 feet

Goodyear Blimp
Length: 192 feet

777 Stretch Passenger Plane
Length: 242 feet

The *Hindenburg* was the biggest airship ever built. It carried passengers across the Atlantic Ocean. In May 1937, the *Hindenburg* was destroyed by fire.

Research

- Find some other information about the *Hindenburg*.
- Find out the height of a very tall building. Compare the height of the building to the length of the *Hindenburg*. What did you discover?

HANGING AROUND

Gliders were developed after years of investigation into the flight of birds and kites. They were the first craft to let people soar through the air like birds.

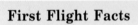

Lilienthal's Number 11 Glider

First Flight Facts

Glider length: 16 feet, 5 inches

Wingspan: 22 feet, 11 inches

Weight: 44 pounds

Altitude reached: 33 feet

Distance flown: about 985 feet

In 1891, after 20 years of investigating how birds fly, Otto Lilienthal became the first person to build and fly a glider. Lilienthal made more than 2,000 successful flights in his gliders, and became known as the world's first true aviator.

Like Lilienthal's first gliders, modern hang gliders are steered by shifting body weight from side to side. They are called hang gliders because the person "hangs" beneath the wing.

Fact Sheet: a modern hang glider

Length: 10 feet

Wingspan: 33 feet, 4 inches

Weight: 66 pounds

Altitude: 25,000 feet

In 1849 it was claimed that a young boy crossed a small valley in this glider. It would have been an amazing flight if it really occurred; there was no way of steering the glider, and the flapping wings could not have lifted it.

23

SILENT SAILING

Hang gliders are not the only aircraft that soar through the air without using engines.

A Modern Sailplane

- A sailplane is a kind of glider. To gain altitude, a pilot of a hang glider or sailplane must find a current of rising warm air, known as a *thermal*.
- A sailplane has flown as high as 42,303 feet. How does this compare with the "high flyers" shown on page 16?

A sailplane pilot might follow a flight plan using compass directions and landmarks. Look at the aerial photograph on page 25.

1. What direction do you fly from:
   a. the airport to the swamp?
   b. the airport to the fairgrounds?
   c. Long Bridge to Taylor Bridge?
2. Follow this flight plan. Where do you get to?
   Fly East from the airport for one mile. Turn North and fly for 2 miles. Turn West and fly for 2 miles. Then fly Southwest for $2\frac{1}{2}$ miles.
3. Make up a flight plan for a friend to follow.

To get into the air, a sailplane can be towed behind another plane, then released when it is high enough.

Aerial Photograph   Scale: 1 inch = 1 mile

Using a grid

The grid position of the airport is 4C. What is the grid position of:

a. the swamp?   **b.** Taylor Bridge?

PROPELLER PLANES

The first airplanes were fragile machines. They were made almost entirely of wood and cloth, held together with wire. The engines were small, but they turned large propellers. Most importantly, these early airplanes flew!

First Flight Facts

Airplane length: 21 feet, 1 inch

Wingspan: 40 feet, 4 inches

Propeller diameter: 8 feet, 6 inches

Take-off weight: 750 pounds

Altitude: 12 feet

Top speed: 29 miles per hour

Distance flown: 170 feet

Flight time: 12 seconds

Orville and Wilbur Wright made history on December 17, 1903, with the first airplane flight. Their plane *The Flyer* flew for 12 seconds. It was powered by a gasoline engine connected to two propellers by bicycle chains.

The 777 Stretch plane is longer than the entire length of *The Flyer's* first flight.

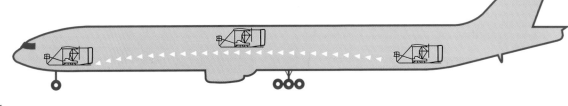

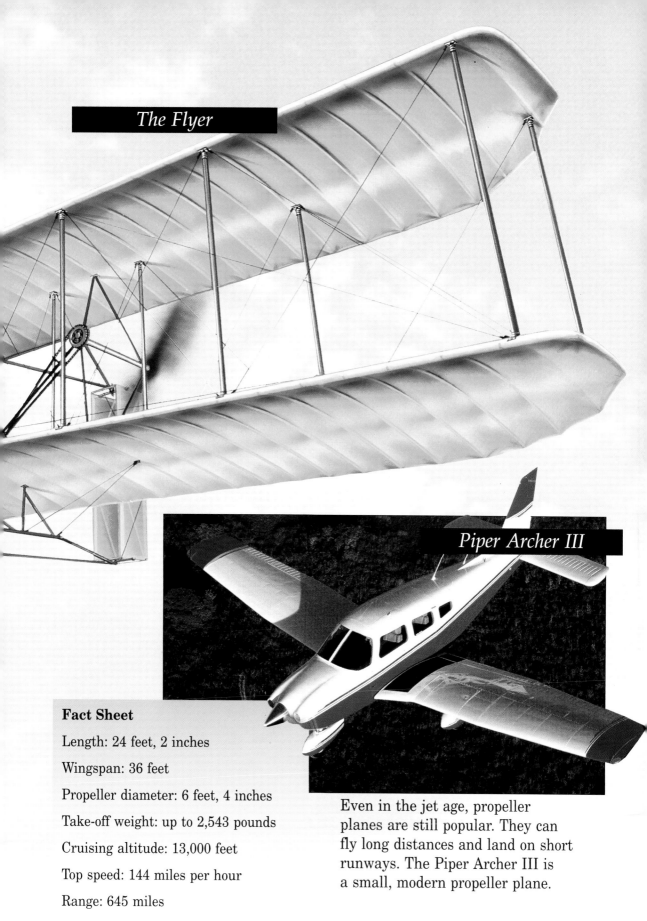

The Flyer

Piper Archer III

Fact Sheet

Length: 24 feet, 2 inches

Wingspan: 36 feet

Propeller diameter: 6 feet, 4 inches

Take-off weight: up to 2,543 pounds

Cruising altitude: 13,000 feet

Top speed: 144 miles per hour

Range: 645 miles

Even in the jet age, propeller planes are still popular. They can fly long distances and land on short runways. The Piper Archer III is a small, modern propeller plane.

THE SPRUCE GOOSE

Flying boats, or seaplanes, are planes that are designed to take off from water and land on water. The *Spruce Goose* is a giant wooden flying boat – the largest propeller plane ever to fly.

1. Compare the first flights of the *Spruce Goose* and *The Flyer*. Which plane flew farther? How much farther?
2. How much longer is the wingspan of the *Spruce Goose* than:
   a. the wingspan of *The Flyer*?
   b. the wingspan of a Piper Archer III?
3. a. Which plane has a length that is about half its wingspan?
   b. How long would the *Spruce Goose* be if its length was half its wingspan?

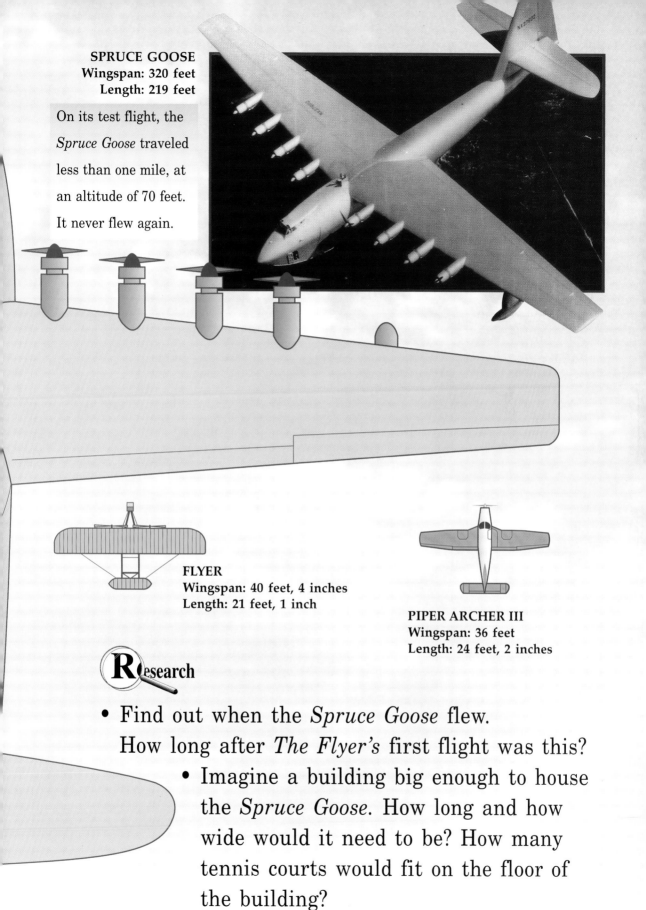

SPRUCE GOOSE
Wingspan: 320 feet
Length: 219 feet

On its test flight, the *Spruce Goose* traveled less than one mile, at an altitude of 70 feet. It never flew again.

FLYER
Wingspan: 40 feet, 4 inches
Length: 21 feet, 1 inch

PIPER ARCHER III
Wingspan: 36 feet
Length: 24 feet, 2 inches

Research

- Find out when the *Spruce Goose* flew. How long after *The Flyer's* first flight was this?

  - Imagine a building big enough to house the *Spruce Goose*. How long and how wide would it need to be? How many tennis courts would fit on the floor of the building?

Jetting Around

Many planes today have jet engines instead of propellers. These engines suck in air and push it out behind them. This thrusts the plane forward. Jets can carry passengers and cargo faster and farther than any propeller plane.

Boeing 777 Stretch

The longest passenger airplane in the world is the Boeing 777 Stretch. It is 10 feet 6 inches longer than the Jumbo Jet, which had held the record since 1969.

Fact Sheet

Length: 242 feet, 4 inches

Wingspan: 199 feet, 11 inches

Take-off weight: 660,000 pounds

Top speed: 530 miles per hour

Range: 6,550 miles

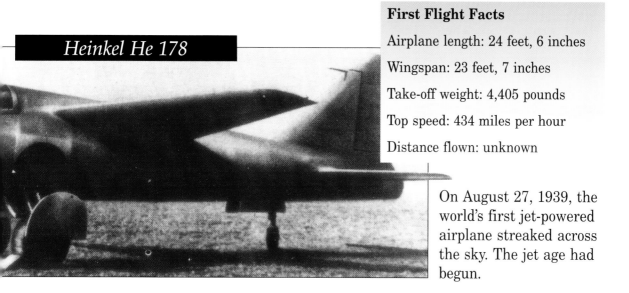

Heinkel He 178

First Flight Facts

Airplane length: 24 feet, 6 inches

Wingspan: 23 feet, 7 inches

Take-off weight: 4,405 pounds

Top speed: 434 miles per hour

Distance flown: unknown

On August 27, 1939, the world's first jet-powered airplane streaked across the sky. The jet age had begun.

Concorde

- Sound travels in air at about 650 miles per hour. When an aircraft travels faster than this, it is said to "break the sound barrier."
- The Concorde is a super fast jet plane. It can reach speeds of 1,307 miles per hour – more than twice the speed of sound. The Concorde can fly from New York to London in only three and a half hours.

SEATING PLANS

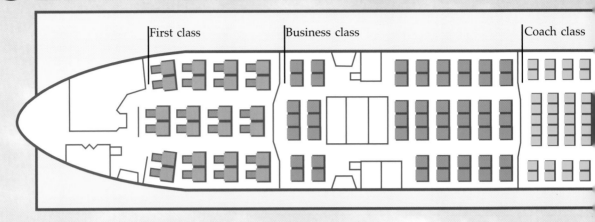

First class · Business class · Coach class

Usually the 777 Stretch has first class, business class, and coach class seats. Sometimes the whole plane has coach class seating; then a 777 can carry up to 550 passengers.

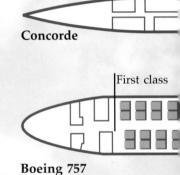

Concorde

Boeing 757

First class

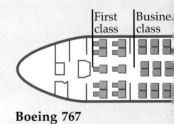

Boeing 767

First class · Busine class

1. a. How many passengers can sit in the three-class 777? Show how you calculated the total.

   b. How many more passengers could sit in a 777 with coach class only?

2. How many more passengers can the three-class 777 carry than:

   a. a 757?

   b. a 767?

3. How many trips would a Concorde need to make to carry all the passengers that a three-class 777 could carry in one trip?

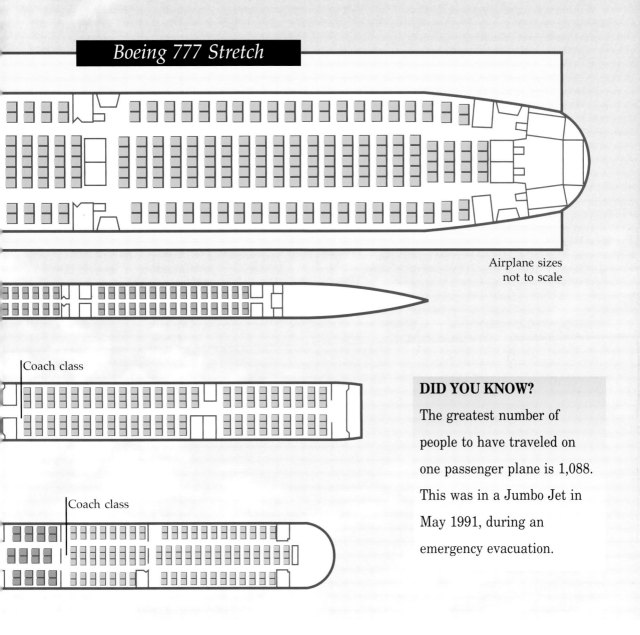

Boeing 777 Stretch

Airplane sizes
not to scale

Coach class

Coach class

Research

- Find out how many passengers a Jumbo Jet can seat.
- Which plane or planes would be needed to carry every student and teacher in your school, with fewest seats left empty?

RACING ROCKETS

Rocket engines are extremely powerful. They produce such great thrust that they can launch heavy vehicles far into space. A spacecraft must carry fuel for the rocket engines, as well as the oxygen that is needed to burn the fuel in space.

Space Shuttle

A space shuttle has rocket engines, but it can land like an ordinary plane. To launch a shuttle into space, massive rockets blast it from Earth at 25 times the speed of sound.

Fact Sheet: shuttle orbiter

Length: 122 feet

Wingspan: 78 feet

Take-off weight: 4,500,000 pounds

Orbiting altitude: up to 600 miles

Speed: up to 17,600 miles per hour

The Goddard Rocket

First Flight Facts

Rocket length: 9 feet, 8 inches

Wingspan: none

Take-off weight: 10 pounds, 6 ounces

Altitude reached: 41 feet

Speed: 60 miles per hour

Professor Robert Goddard was the American pioneer of rocketry. He invented the first successful liquid-fueled rocket, which flew on March 16, 1926.

On October 14, 1947, Charles "Chuck" Yeager became the first pilot to break through the invisible sound barrier. He set this record in a bullet-shaped rocket plane, at an altitude of 43,000 feet.

In and Out of Space

NASA regularly launches shuttles into space.
A shuttle flight has seven major stages.

Launch

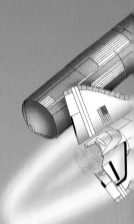

Rocket booster separation
Time from launch: 2 minutes
Altitude: 27 miles
Speed: 3,200 miles per hour

1. How fast does the shuttle travel two minutes after launch? How much faster does it travel eight minutes after launch?

2. A shuttle takes approximately 90 minutes to orbit the Earth. How long would it take to complete:
   a. 2 orbits?
   b. 3 orbits?
   c. 5 orbits?

3. About how many orbits of the Earth would a shuttle complete in:
   a. one day?
   b. 30 days?

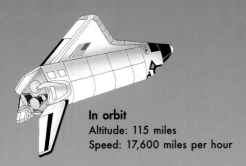

In orbit
Altitude: 115 miles
Speed: 17,600 miles per hour

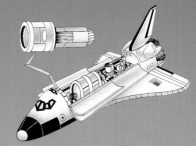

Working in space
Orbiting altitude: 100–600 miles
Duration: up to 30 days

Fuel tank separation
Time from launch:
8 minutes
Altitude: 70 miles
Speed: 17,500 miles per hour

**Coming back into
Earth's atmosphere**
Altitude: 76 miles
Speed: 17,400 miles per hour

DID YOU KNOW?

The first rocket-powered plane
took off years before the first
jet plane or space rocket was
invented. It was called
The Duck and flew on
June 11, 1928.

Landing
Speed: 200 miles per hour

Research

- Find out when the first shuttle flight took place.
  How many years ago was this?
  What was the name of the shuttle?
- A shuttle travels 115 miles to orbiting altitude.
  Find out how much farther a spacecraft would
  have to travel to reach the moon.

AROUND THE WORLD

Not many people will ever get to fly in a rocket, but thousands of people every day experience international jet travel.

VANCOUVER

To Hong Kong 6,901 miles

SAN FRANSCISCO

To Tokyo 5,451 miles

2,572 miles

2,461 miles

LOS ANGELES

NEW YORK

4,713 miles

3,458 miles

3,630 miles

4,799 miles

5,767 mi

To Sydney 7,471 miles

To Auckland 6,490 miles

RIO DE JANEIRO

1,240 miles

To Auckland 6,386 miles

BUENOS AIRES

1. Which flight distance is closest to:
   a. 2,500 miles?
   b. 5,000 miles?
   c. 7,500 miles?
2. **a.** Plan a trip of between 18,000 and 20,000 miles, starting and finishing in New York.
   b. How much flying time would your trip involve? Show how you calculated the total.
3. Plan a trip "around the world," starting in Los Angeles. How does the total distance of your trip compare with the distance around the equator?

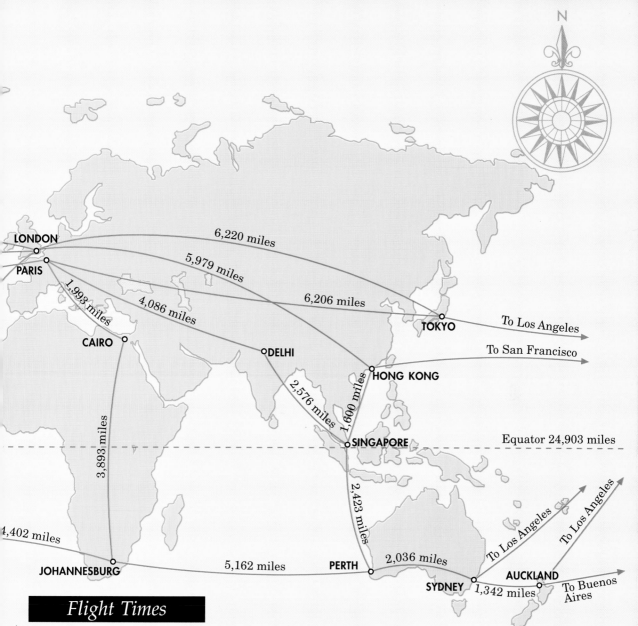

N

LONDON
PARIS
6,220 miles
5,979 miles
6,206 miles
1,993 miles
4,086 miles
CAIRO
DELHI
TOKYO
To Los Angeles
To San Francisco
HONG KONG
2,576 miles
1,600 miles
3,893 miles
SINGAPORE
Equator 24,903 miles
2,423 miles
4,402 miles
To Los Angeles
To Los Angeles
JOHANNESBURG
5,162 miles
PERTH
2,036 miles
AUCKLAND
To Buenos Aires
SYDNEY
1,342 miles

Flight Times

Buenos Aires – Auckland	13 hrs 50 mins	Paris – New York	8 hrs
Cairo – Johannesburg	8 hrs	Paris – Tokyo	12 hrs 25 mins
Cairo – Paris	4 hrs 30 mins	Perth – Johannesburg	9 hrs 5 mins
Hong Kong – San Francisco	12 hrs	Perth – Singapore	4 hrs 40 mins
Johannesburg – Rio de Janeiro	9 hrs 30 mins	Rio de Janeiro – Buenos Aires	3 hrs
London – Hong Kong	13 hrs	Rio de Janeiro – London	11 hrs
London – New York	7 hrs 25 mins	San Francisco – New York	5 hrs 25 mins
London – Vancouver	9 hrs	Singapore – Delhi	5 hrs 15 mins
Los Angeles – Auckland	12 hrs 5 mins	Singapore – Hong Kong	3 hrs 25 mins
Los Angeles – Tokyo	11 hrs 25 mins	Sydney – Auckland	3 hrs
New York – Los Angeles	5 hrs 15 mins	Sydney – Los Angeles	14 hrs 45 mins
New York – Rio de Janeiro	9 hrs 48 mins	Sydney – Perth	4 hrs 50 mins
Paris – Delhi	8 hrs 40 mins	Tokyo – London	12 hrs 30 mins

AIRSHIPS

TIMELINE

● **1852**
Henri Giffard
(France) built and
piloted the first
airship.

● **1884** (France)
Flight of the first
airship to have an
effective steering
system. The airship
was called *La France*.

PROPELLER PLANES

JETS

ROCKETS

1. List some events that occurred in the
   decade between 1930 and 1940.

2. How many years after Henri Giffard's
   airship did each of these fly:
   a. the first propeller plane?
   b. the first jet airplane?
   c. the first rocket airplane?

3. For how many years did airships
   carry passengers across the
   Atlantic Ocean?

4. How many years ago did:
   a. the first airship flight take place?
   b. Amelia Earhart fly across
   the Atlantic?
   c. Yuri Gagarin fly into space?